Nondo was a brown cow. She had lovely, big, curved horns. She had a little bell round her neck.

Nondo lived with all the other cows in a little pen in the village.

Every day Temba, the little cowherd, took Nondo and the other cows out of the pen.
They went in search of grass to eat.
They went to the big river to drink.

All the cows followed Nondo because her bell went jingle jangle as she walked.

Temba heard the bell too and he always knew where Nondo was.

Temba loved Nondo very much, because she was a gentle cow.

He liked to stroke her soft nose or put his face against her warm neck. Then he shared his mealie with her as a treat.

One hot, summer day Nondo led the other cows down to the river.
The girls and women were doing their washing on the rocks.

Temba watched the cows all morning. After that he felt very hot, so he decided to have a swim in the river.

First he paddled and splashed near the rocks. The water felt wonderful.

Temba laughed as he splashed about and jumped around on the rocks. The women and girls watched him.

Suddenly he fell into a deep pool. The river was flowing quickly and the rushing water carried Temba away from the rocks.

The women screamed.

Nondo was drinking when she heard them. She looked up and saw Temba in the river. The water was carrying him farther away.

Nondo jumped into the river.

Nondo struggled towards Temba and at last she reached him. She put her head down. Temba caught hold of her long horns.

Slowly, slowly Nondo backed through the water until she reached the bank. Temba held on tightly to Nondo's horns. He was trembling with fright.

When Nondo reached the bank, Temba climbed out of the water. He was shivering.

'Oh, thank you, thank you, Nondo,' he cried. He put his arms round Nondo's neck.

The women stood and shouted, 'Aiee, aiee!' Someone gave Temba a towel.

They all came to praise Nondo. 'Oh, Nondo,' said a girl. 'You've lost your bell!'

That night everyone in the village heard the story. The blacksmith said, 'I will make a new bell for Nondo.'

People came to look at Nondo. Temba told them the story again and again.

'We must have a big party tonight,' said Temba's father. So they did.

Everyone in the village came and danced all night.

At midnight Temba went to Nondo's pen. He gave her some of her favourite food, groundnut leaves and mealie stalks. He put the big new bell round her neck.

'Thank you, Nondo,' he said.

HOP STEP JUMP

In My Father's Village   Michael Palmer
Striped Paint   Rosina Umelo
The Slow Chameleon and **Shammy's Bride**   David Cobb
The Walking Talking Flying ABC   David Cobb

Choose Me!   Lynn Kramer
Nondo the Cow   Diane Rasteiro
Sika in the Snow   David Cobb

Chichi and the Termites   Wendy Ijioma
The Boy who ate a Hyena   James G D Ngumy
Tickets for the Zed Band   Lynn Kramer

© Copyright text Diane Rasteiro 1992
© Copyright illustrations The Macmillan Press Ltd 1992

All rights reserved. No reproduction, copy or transmission of this publication may be made without written permission.

No paragraph of this publication may be reproduced, copied or transmitted save with written permission or in accordance with the provisions of the Copyright, Designs and Patents Act 1988, or under the terms of any licence permitting limited copying issued by the Copyright Licensing Agency, 90 Tottenham Court Road, London W1P 9HE.

Any person who does any unauthorised act in relation to this publication may be liable to criminal prosecution and civil claims for damages.

First published 1992

Published by THE MACMILLAN PRESS LTD
London and Basingstoke
Associated companies and representatives in Accra, Auckland, Delhi, Dublin, Gaborone, Hamburg, Harare, Hong Kong, Kuala Lumpur, Lagos, Manzini, Melbourne, Mexico City, Nairobi, New York, Singapore, Tokyo.

ISBN 0-333-57655-1

Printed in Hong Kong

A catalogue record for this book is available from the British Library.

Illustrations by Felicity Cary